Other books from *The Sun*:

John Steadman: Days In The Sun,
    by John Steadman

Off Season,
    by Susan White-Bowden and Jack Bowden

Postcards of Maryland: Sports

Goal: A history of the Baltimore Blast indoor soccer team

Miss Prudence Pennypack's Perfectly Proper,
    by Karen Rupprecht

Marylanders Of The Century,
    edited by Barry Rascovar

Are We There Yet? Recollections Of Life's Many Journeys,
    by Elise T. Chisolm

A Century In The Sun: Photographs Of Maryland
    edited by Joseph R.L. Sterne

A Century In The Sun: Front Pages Of The Twentieth Century

A Century In The Sun: Postcards Of Maryland's Past

Hometown Boy: The Hoodle Patrol And Other Curiosities Of Baltimore,
    by Rafael Alvarez

The Great Game of Maryland Politics,
    by Barry Rascovar

Other books by Kevin Kallaugher:

KAL Draws A Crowd, Woodholme House, 1997

KALtoons, Chatsworth Press, 1992

Drawn from the Economist, The Economist Publications, 1988

This Baltimore Sun book was published by SunSource, the information service of *The Sun*. To order any of the above titles published by The Baltimore Sun or for information on research, reprints and information from the paper's archives, please call 410.332.6800 or visit www.sunspot.net/sunsource.

KAL
draws the line

Political cartoons by Kevin Kallaugher

THE BALTIMORE SUN

Published by
The Baltimore Sun
501 N. Calvert Street, Baltimore, MD 21278
410-332-6800 / www.sunspot.net/sunsource/

M. William Salganik, editor
Jennifer Halbert, layout and design
Ray Frager, copy editor

Photos of Mr. Kallaugher by Jeffrey F. Bill
All photos in this book from *The Sun*, ©2000. All rights reserved.

All cartoons in this book are from *The Sun* and *The Economist*,
© 1996, 1997, 1998, 1999, 2000.

ISBN — 1-893116-18-2
Library of Congress Control Number 00-133239

Kevin Kallaugher's cartoons are distributed exclusively by
Cartoonists & Writers Syndicate
67 Riverside Drive, New York, N.Y. 10024
212-362-9256 / 212-595-4218 fax / cws@cartoonweb.com

KAL draws the line — 2000 — Baltimore, MD: Baltimore Sun Co.: 2000

To Joe,
who believed enough in a young cartoonist
to bring him from Britain to Baltimore

Contents

Foreword

Yeah, yeah, yeah. Everybody loves a good cartoon. Except, of course, the subject of the cartoon.

Just why did Kal pick me to write this introduction? Haven't I been punished enough?

First of all, I **do not** have jowls. Second of all, I **do not** have a double chin.

However, Kal (whose real name, I find out, is the rather uninteresting Kevin Kallaugher) **does** have a double chin.

But I suppose there is art even where there is adversity. And certainly Kal is an artist.

Whatever. Good luck and may God bless you, Kal. I expect regular royalty checks.

William Donald Schaefer,
a reluctant admirer
May, 2000

Introduction

by Kevin Kallaugher

"A good caricature, like every work of art, is more true to life than reality itself."

— Annibale Carrachi, Italian Renaissance painter, 1560-1609

To me, one of the most enjoyable challenges of being an editorial cartoonist is trying to create and master the caricature of a politician. Endeavoring to capture the face and the personality behind it in a distorted yet recognizable form is a process that has fascinated me for more than 30 years.

The first caricature I remember drawing was of a fifth-grade music teacher. She was an enthusiastic nun who had the habit of singing in utter rapture with her eyes firmly shut. One day while the sister was in full choral flow, I seized the moment to capture her on paper. I gave her a little button nose, curly hair, slits for eyes ... and a mouth open wide enough to fit a battleship.

The cartoon was soon, surreptitiously, finding its way around the classroom. To my excitement, it was met with copious giggles and guffaws. The inevitable discovery by the singing nun of the offending drawing changed the class' mood dramatically. I was summarily marched down to the boys lavatory by the teacher. There, she stood over me and ordered me to take

1992

1993

a bite out of a bar of soap. "Don't you ever draw another cartoon like that again!" she bellowed.

I've been drawing them ever since.

Today, when I draw a personality, I don't often get as close to my target as I did in 5th grade music class. Instead, I have to rely on photographs, television and, increasingly, the Internet, to supply me with the images from which I can gain inspiration.

In the early stages of drawing a new political figure, the caricature closely resembles the photographs. Over time, the caricatures become increasingly daring, distorted and ridiculous. In some cases, the cartoons become so oversimplified that if you placed a photograph of a personality next to his or her caricature, you would be hard-pressed to see a resemblance. However, standing on its own, the caricature is widely recognized as being the intended target.

This is because the cartoon audience has learned over time what cartoon features symbolize which politician: Nixon's heavy brow and ski slope nose, Reagan's wrinkles, pompadour and goofy grin, Clinton's jutting chin and bulbous nose.

My rendition of Bill Clinton has evolved dramatically over the nine years that I have struggled with his face. My first attempt was in 1991 when then-Gov. Clinton had yet to launch his White House bid. The cartoon was based on one grainy photo of a small-time governor that I had never seen before and never expected to see again. The drawing (on this page) speaks, rather poorly, for itself.

1991

1995

1998

As Bill Clinton ascended to the White House, I explored and experimented with his face with mixed success. I tinkered with the formula ... making the eyes smaller or the hair taller, adding more bags under the eyes or more width to the jaw. It is a curious process of trial and error, all the time searching for a magic formula of recognition.

I try not to make a habit of drawing a politician's caricature the same way every time. I aspire to make his or her face fit the mood and the demands of the cartoon in which they are situated. If, for example, Bill Clinton is in a drawing where he is championing the rights of the poor, I might portray him in a more flattering light than I might if he was, say, having an affair with a White House intern.

1997

After hundreds of attempts at drawing Bill Clinton, I think that I have just now captured him. I now know his face so well that I can draw a reasonable rendition of him from all angles in a variety of styles ... from memory.

So I lament the end of the Clinton era, as I did the end of the Reagan and Bush eras. Having trained arduously for many years to effectively caricature the presidents, I think it is rather inconsiderate of them to leave office.

But that is all right.

In the caricature business, there are two things that are certain. One, more politicians will step into the breach and supply a cornucopia of material from which to draw inspiration.

Two, I'll never go into a boys lavatory with a nun again.

1999

2000

National affairs

It was, it seemed, all about money. A booming economy — symbolized by dot-com millionaires and behemoth gas-guzzlers — helped produce the first balanced budget since 1969. With money available, some in Congress pressed for tax cuts, while others sought new programs. Away from the Capitol, the economy had its impact on society, and it wasn't all positive.

September 1, 1998
The vibrant economy helped keep Bill Clinton popular ...

February 2, 1999
... and kept the federal government awash in cash.

December 26, 1998
A dwindling few believed warnings that the economic bubble was about to burst.

October 5, 1999

Deadlocked on many fiscal issues, congressional Democrats and Republicans found one on which they could unite.

6

October 1, 1998
Some wanted to harvest the government's new-found wealth.

November 25, 1999

The budget that finally emerged was stuffed with spending projects in the districts of powerful legislators.

July 1, 1999
Below the surface, problems lurked.

June 14, 1998
Not all benefited from the prosperity.

RELAX! WHAT COULD GO WRONG HERE IN "Mergerassic Park"?

April 14, 1998
The late '90s had the largest business mergers in history.

March 7, 1998
The government brought an antitrust case against software giant Microsoft.

January 11, 2000
The sudden explosion of commerce in cyberspace created hopes and fears.

March 26, 1998
The relationship of media to violence ...

March 5, 2000
... remained a concern.

April 29, 1999
Incidents such as the massacre at a Littleton, Colo., high school ...

August 1, 1999

... were an occasion for short-lived soul-searching.

May 25, 1998
Old ways remained, sadly, entrenched.

December 7, 1997
President Clinton promised a dialogue on race issues.

November 9, 1997
Republicans sought to end affirmative-action programs.

April 4, 1998
Some barriers proved difficult to breach.

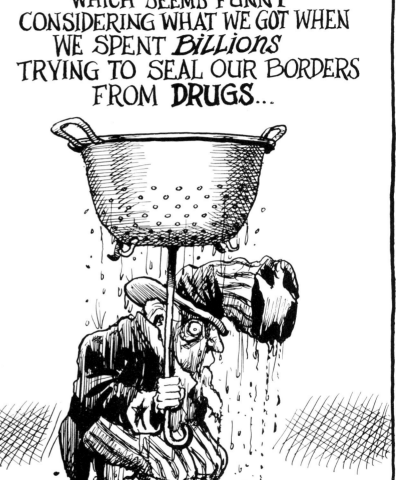

March 21, 1999

The government considered reviving the "star wars" missile defense plan.

June 21, 1997
Officials remained focused on drug interdiction, not drug treatment.

November 22, 1997
As the Dow Jones index grew, so did the size of cars.

March 18, 2000
When gas prices spiked, America reacted.

December 19, 1999
The environment faced long-term challenges.

August 17, 1997
There was pollution in the air ...

August 3, 1999
... there was global warming ...

September 16, 1997

... and there was pollution of waterways.

October 18, 1997
Cost-slashing HMOs created a jarring ride for patients.

July 26, 1998
Politicians debated how best to control HMO excesses.

December 9, 1999
A federal study directed attention to deadly medical errors.

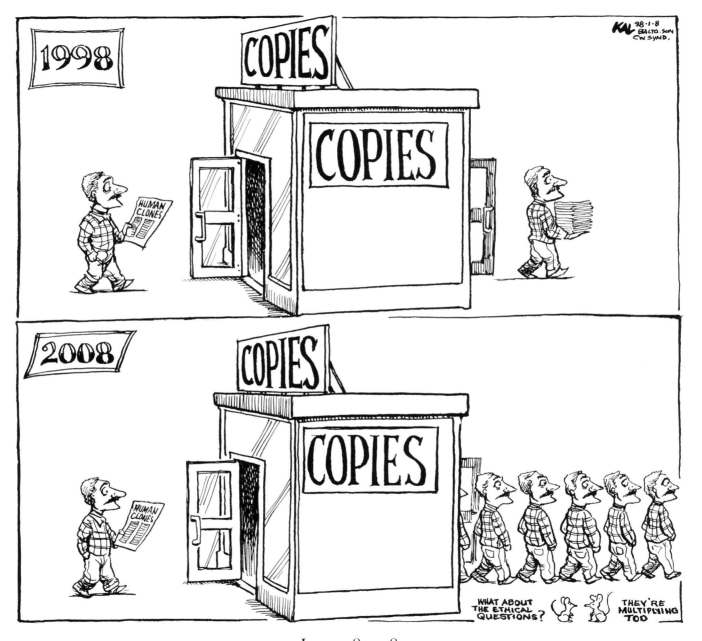

January 8, 1998
Scientists approached a revolution in biology with research in cloning and gene-mapping.

March 10, 1998
To settle court cases, Big Tobacco began paying big money to governments.

February 28, 1999
After the tobacco cases, plaintiffs' lawyers found other industries to sue.

November 27, 1998

Meanwhile, the tobacco companies looked for friendlier places to sell their products.

July 26, 1999
An anniversary Woodstock concert revealed a generation gap.

July 12, 1997

The government's role in support of the National Endowment for the Arts continued to be controversial.

December 16, 1999
The creator of "Peanuts," Charles M. Schulz, died soon after announcing his retirement and drawing his last strip.

December 26, 1999
Round numbers on the calendar produced a feeling of a new era.

Oval Office affairs

A hero-less cast of characters — Bill Clinton, Kenneth Starr, Monica Lewinsky, Linda Tripp, Lucianne Goldberg — dominated the national stage for a year. The overlong play never quite reached a dramatic climax. The public said it was bored with details of phone sex, thong underwear and cigars — but kept watching.

January 25, 1998
Clinton issued denials ...

August 1, 1998

... and attempted to divert attention ...

May 1, 1998
... and tried to change the subject.

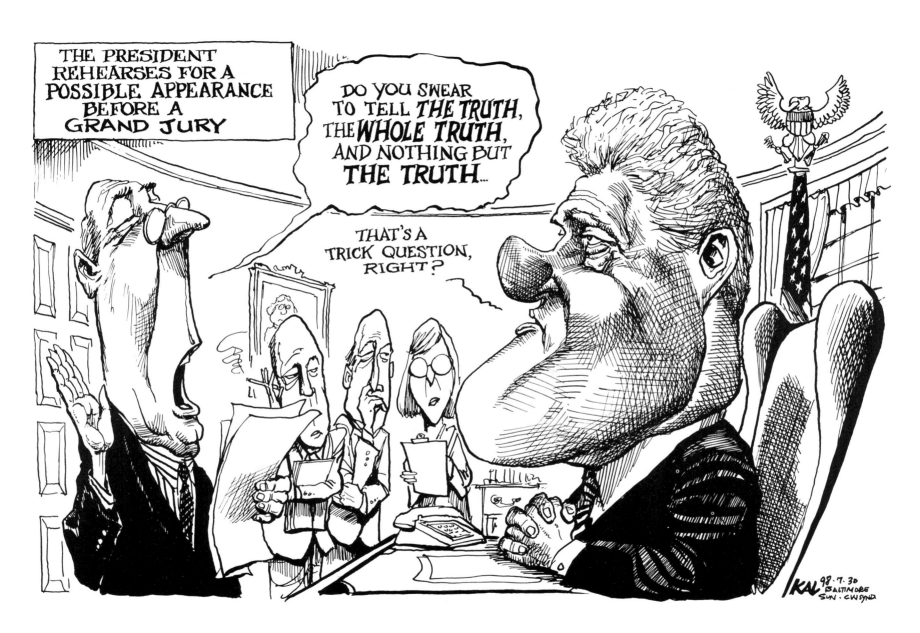

July 30, 1998
The president's lawyerly answers aroused suspicion and ridicule.

July 5, 1999
When the scandal got hot, Clinton made foreign trips.

March 3, 1998
Special Prosecutor Ken Starr zealously pursued his prey.

August 18, 1998
Clinton stood his ground.

September 20, 1998
The Starr Report was full of salacious details.

November 19, 1998
In the end, Starr's case was less impressive than advertised.

August 18, 1998
The president continued to deny.

December 20, 1998
Clinton resisted suggestions that he step down.

IMPEACHMENT
HEARING

December 1, 1998
A weary public tuned out ...

February 5, 1998
... at least some of the time.

September 9, 1998
Some distractions were welcome, including Mark McGwire's home run record.

October 6, 1998

Republicans and Democrats grappled over how Clinton would be remembered.

THE IMPEACHMENT SKATING TRIAL

The HOUSE

SENATE

DANGER THIN CASE

January 3, 1999
Congressional Republicans had trouble finding firm footing ...

January 16, 1999
... *while Democrats found it hard to justify Clinton's behavior.*

December 10, 1998
In the end, the GOP fell short.

August 16, 1998
An impeachment overview.

February 11, 1999
The final vote was dubbed "the moment of truth."

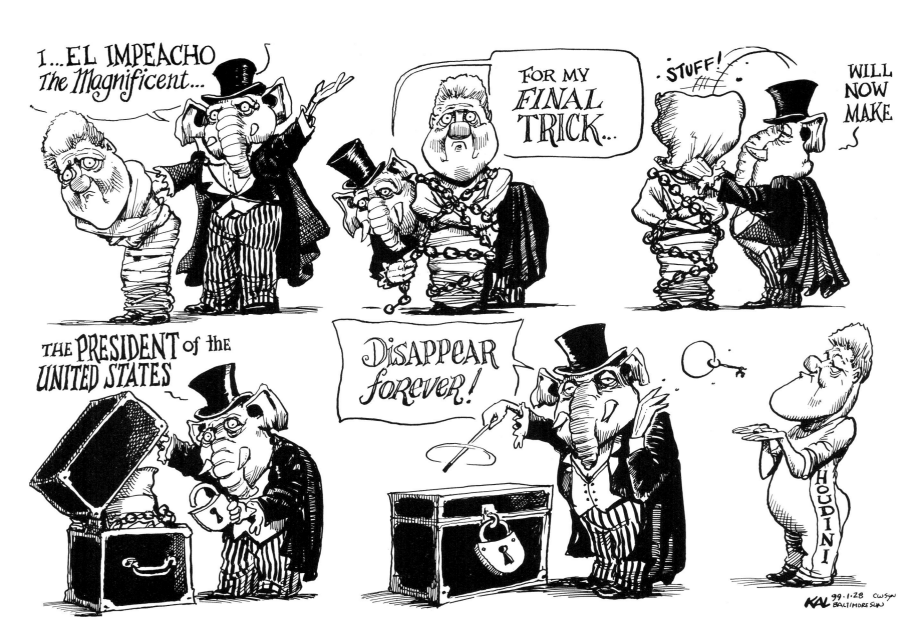

January 28, 1999
The president escaped ...

February 13, 1999
... earning the admiration of some.

February 18, 1999
The Republicans were not left without a Clinton target ...

January 1, 2000
... *as Hillary Clinton decided to run for Senate from New York.*

Political affairs

Front-runners with familiar political names, Al Gore and George W. Bush entered the 2000 presidential campaign season as strong favorites. Both wound up facing vigorous challenges. Both found the need to redefine themselves as they went along. And both eventually wrapped up the nominations early in a process that put a premium on big-time fund-raising.

October 31, 1999
Early predictions gave little regard to potential challengers to Gore and Bush.

July 4, 1999
George W. Bush raised record amounts ...

April 4, 1999
... while the Democrats struggled to keep pace.

July 20, 1998
Campaign cash threatened to dominate the process.

June 29, 1999

Gore seemed unsure whether to distance himself from the Clinton scandals or tie himself to the Clinton prosperity.

June 13, 1999
When Bush entered the campaign, it appeared only one man could stop him.

August 19, 1999

He faced the inevitable questions from a scandal-hardened press.

September 18, 1999
Unable to build support among Republicans, Pat Buchanan switched to Ross Perot's Reform Party.

February 1, 2000
Candidates and their image-builders converged on New Hampshire for the first primary.

January 16, 2000
The one-on-one campaigning in New Hampshire would give way to mass media appeals in larger states.

February 3, 2000

John McCain won among New Hampshire's anti-establishment voters, but Bush had strong organizations elsewhere.

March 16, 1999

Two wooden campaigners led to expectations of a dull contest on the Democratic side.

December 21, 1999
When the cerebral Bradley gained support, Gore switched tactics.

February 17, 2000
The Republican contest heated up as well, as candidates attacked each other in South Carolina.

February 29, 2000
Negative campaigning was offensive but effective.

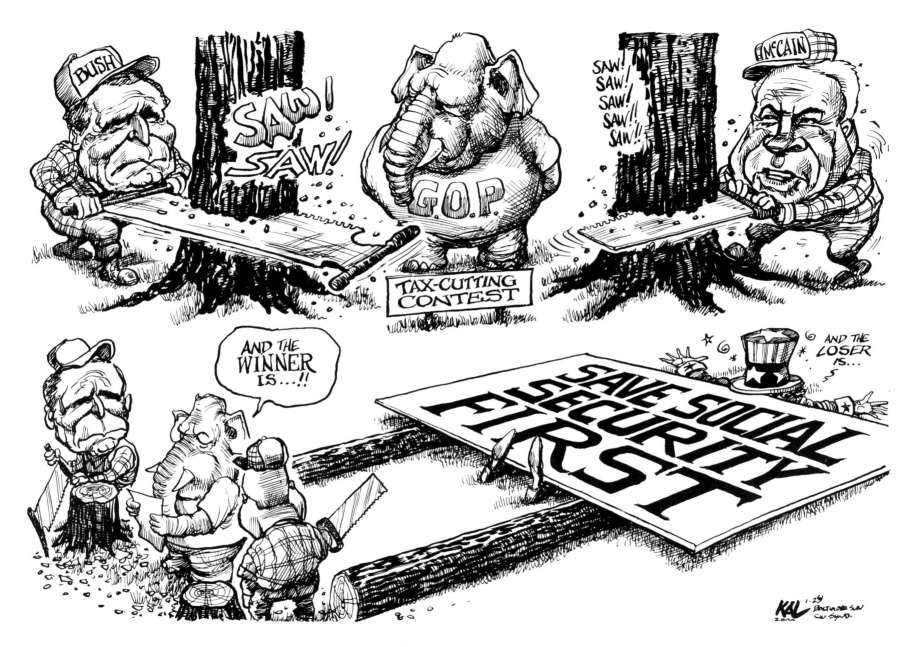

January 24, 2000
Republicans offered tax cut plans, rather than concentrating on programs.

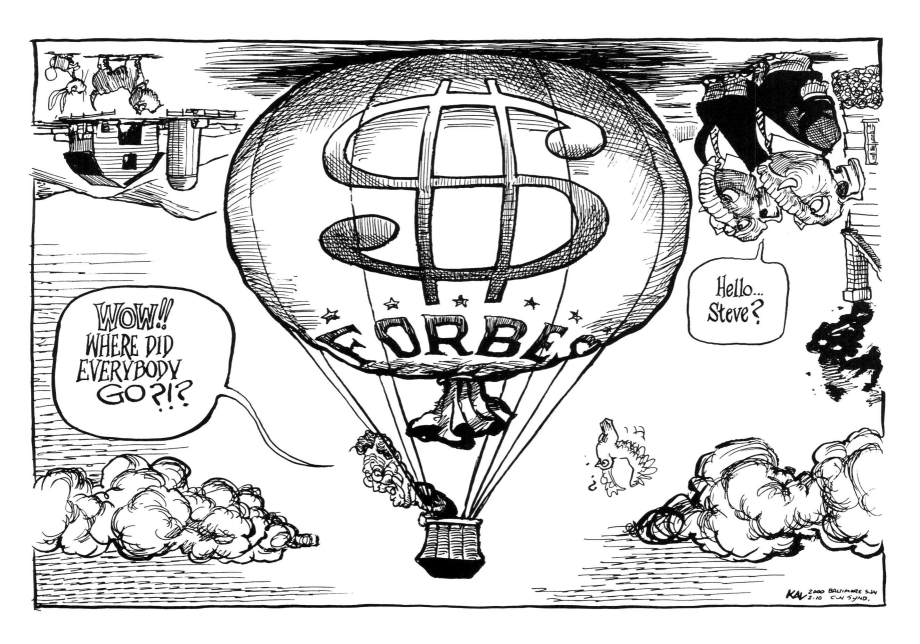

February 10, 2000
Steve Forbes spent millions of his own dollars, and won dozens of Republican votes.

March 9, 2000
In the end, the front-runners were triumphant.

March 28, 2000

When candidates weren't busy raising campaign contributions, they argued about how to limit them.

January 30, 2000
Bush found himself caught between his party's moderates and conservatives.

October 1, 1998
The parties chose their positions.

GEORGE W. BUSH IMPLORES HIS PARTY TO REFASHION ITS IMAGE...

OH, YES!! BABY!! THAT IS SO MUCH MORE ~ YOU!

Compassion Coiffeurs

G.O.P. CONGRESS

October 6, 1999

Trumpeting himself as a "compassionate conservative," Bush sought to reinvent the Republican party.

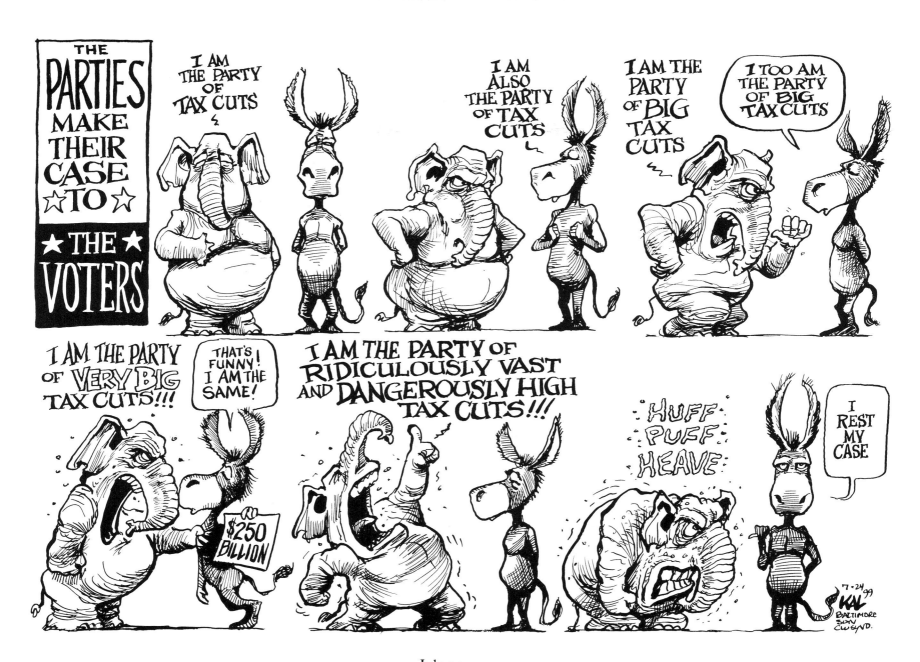

July 24, 1999

Democrats argued for modest tax cuts, claiming the larger Republican cuts would endanger popular programs.

September 14, 1999

A minority of eligible voters made the decisions.

Foreign affairs

The United States solidified its position as The World's Only Superpower, but, despite the occasional bombing run, seemed unable to control a series of annoying little dictators. Serbian hardman Slobodan Milosevic assumed the role of chief villain, although facing tough competition from the usual suspects — perennial contenders Saddam Hussein and Fidel Castro. Besides dictators, Bill Clinton also grappled with the large policy issues — relations with Russia and China, peace in the Mideast — but progress remained elusive.

January 23, 1999
Saddam Hussein and Slobodan Milosevic enjoyed needling their Western adversaries.

November 12, 1998
Saddam proved to be a resilient villain.

February 22, 1998
Frustrated, President Clinton hatched a bombing plan.

February 17, 1998
It was unclear the bombs would produce the desired effect.

February 19, 1998
Bombs did not get Saddam to behave.

November 11, 1997
Sanctions were ineffective as well.

June 10, 1998
Similarly, Milosevic held on ...

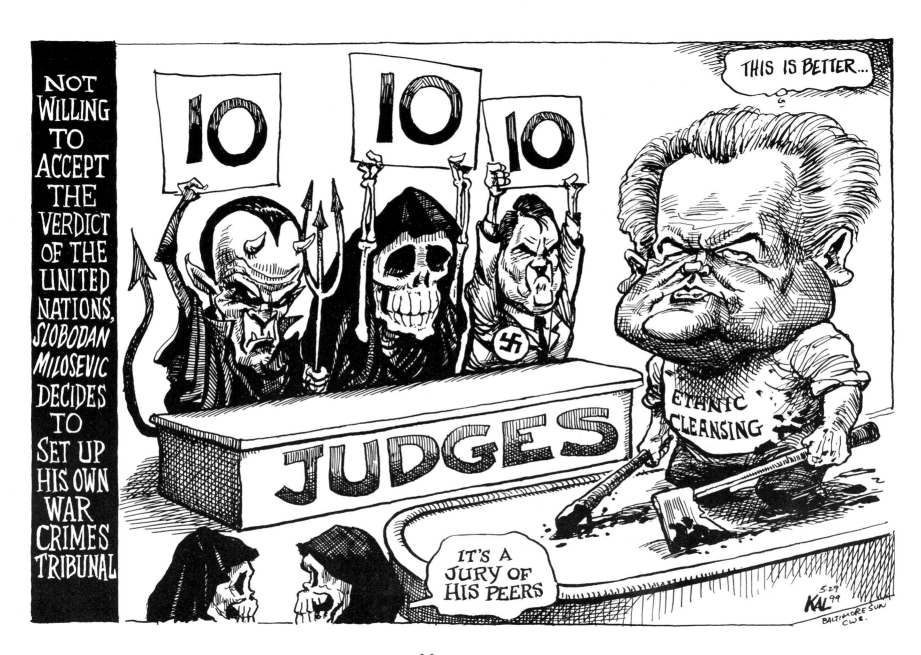

May 29, 1999
... despite war crimes tribunals ...

April 10, 1999
... and NATO bombing raids.

June 5, 1999
Serbia exited a decimated Kosovo. NATO peacekeepers entered.

July 3, 1999
It became clear the mission was becoming a long-term one.

February 25, 1999
Diplomacy also failed to calm the situation.

April 13, 1999
For Clinton, there was neither victory nor escape.

January 5, 1999

A few years in the Balkans seemed like nothing compared to the long standoff with Cuba.

January 28, 2000
The shipwreck of Elian Gonzalez added a new twist to U.S.-Cuba discussions.

April 8, 2000

The Cuban-American community clung to the young Elian as a symbol ...

January 8, 2000

... *creating for the two governments, oddly, a common bond.*

SHAKE

VIETNAM

APPLYING CONSISTENCY TO Foreign POLICY

KAL 3·14 2000 BALTIMORE SUN·CWSYND.

SHAKE

CUBA

March 14, 2000
While continuing to confront Castro, the U.S. was reaching out to other communist countries.

March 25, 1999
Clinton tried to present a coherent foreign policy.

February 27, 2000

Despite an escalation of tension over Taiwan, the administration remained conciliatory toward China.

November 29, 1997
The U.S. economy boomed, while Japan's fizzled.

March 21, 2000
Seeking to bring historic antagonists together, Clinton visited South Asia ...

October 20, 1998
... and devoted considerable efforts to the divided Mideast.

October 24, 1998
Talks broke off and resumed, without ever reaching the critical final stage.

March 25, 2000
The status of Jerusalem remained a key unresolved issue.

119

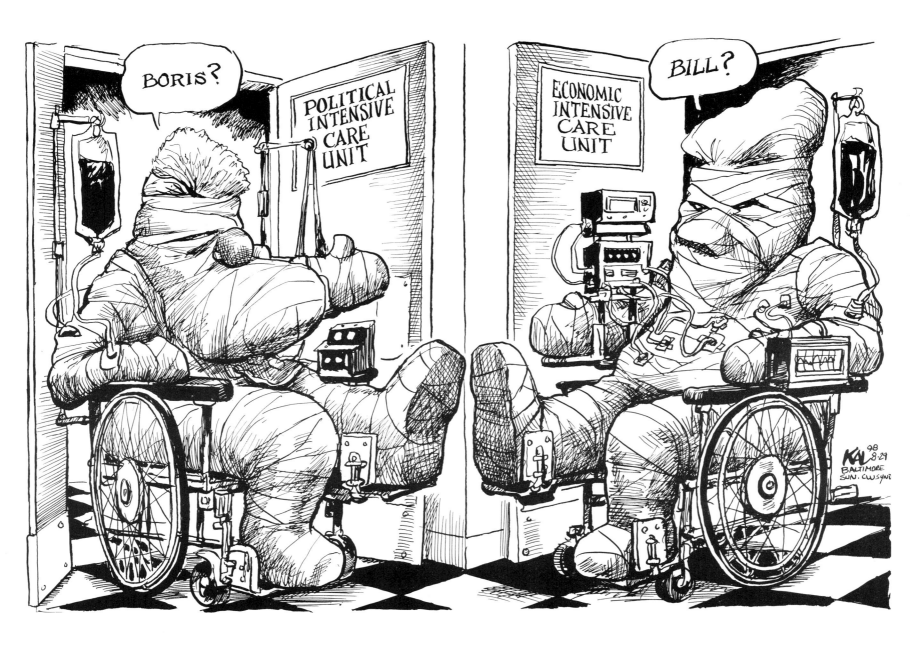

August 29, 1998

Straightjacketed by impeachment politics, Bill Clinton found an ally in Russian president Boris Yeltsin.

February 13, 2000

Yeltsin's Millennium-eve resignation brought former spy agency chief Vladimir Putin to center stage.

October 16, 1999
The U.S. Senate failed to ratify the nuclear test ban treaty.

July 8, 1997
Foreign policy became a low priority in post-Cold War America.

April 28, 1998

In Europe, right-wing nationalism stirred troubling memories.

February 20, 2000

Peace efforts in Northern Ireland continued to be plagued by those who would not abandon the old mistrusts.

April 13, 1998

Pol Pot, who presided over the brutal "killing fields" of Cambodia in the 1970s, died a natural death after years in hiding.

December 6, 1998
International efforts to protect human rights faced persistent opposition.

March 18, 1999
The International Olympic Committee tried to put the best face on scandals surrounding bids to hold the games.

November 30, 1999

The arcane workings of the World Trade Organization suddenly became a subject of widespread protest.

May 11, 1999

The administration was more comfortable with domestic rather than foreign policy issues ...

August 12, 1998
... *while many Americans had other priorities.*

131

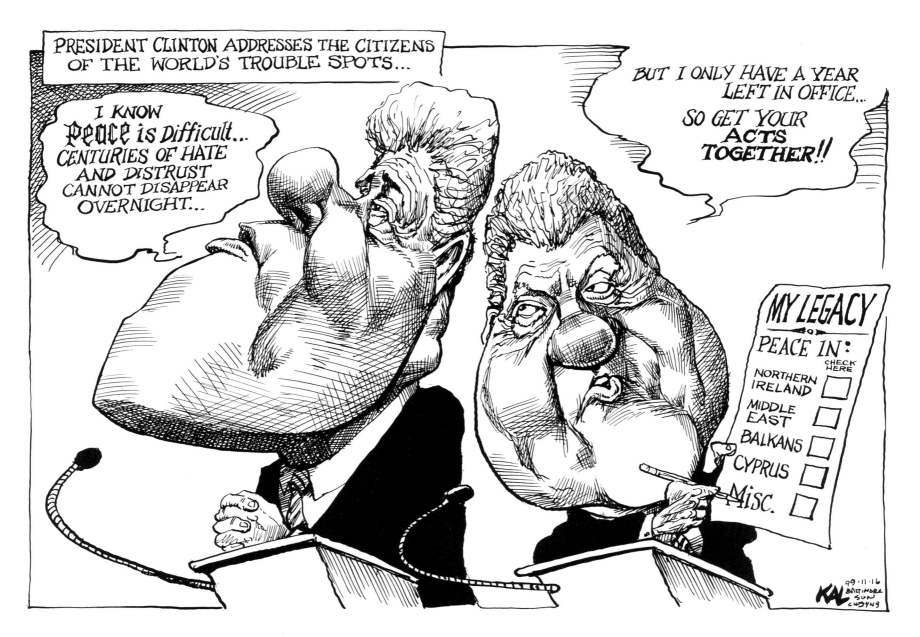

November 16, 1999

Clinton spent his last year touring the world, seeking to polish his resume.

Local affairs

MARYLAND TERRAPIN
2000

In Maryland, it was a time of continuity and discontinuity. Parris Glendening, better known for his lack of charisma than for any particular policies or achievements, faced a tough re-election fight, but won a second term. Like the governor, certain issues — crime and guns, education, traffic — managed to hang around. In contrast, however, a dispirited Mayor Kurt Schmoke decided not to run for re-election in Baltimore, and an energetic Martin O'Malley emerged from the pack to win the mayor's office.

September 27, 1998

Having edged Ellen Sauerbrey in 1994, Parris Glendening headed into a 1998 rematch with tepid support.

August 11, 1998

Baltimore Mayor Kurt Schmoke backed Eileen Rehrmann in the primary, but she pulled out of the race.

October 11, 1998

Eventually, Schmoke endorsed Glendening, but with something less than enthusiasm.

January 22, 1998
A state surplus was perfect for campaign promises.

July 23, 1998
At first Glendening and Sauerbrey seemed evenly matched.

August 25, 1998
Sauerbrey's environmental stands were criticized.

June 21, 1998
Seeking to appeal to centrist voters, Sauerbrey picked a more palatable running mate.

141

October 28, 1998
Voters were treated to a double dose of attack ads.

August 30, 1998
While Glendening struggled past Sauerbrey, William Donald Schaefer waltzed to a coronation.

January 21, 1999
With the former governor in the comptroller's office, there was not always harmony.

December 11, 1997
When attention was brought belatedly to his ethical lapses, State Sen. Larry Young was ousted.

March 7, 1999
Still, legislators resisted ethics reform.

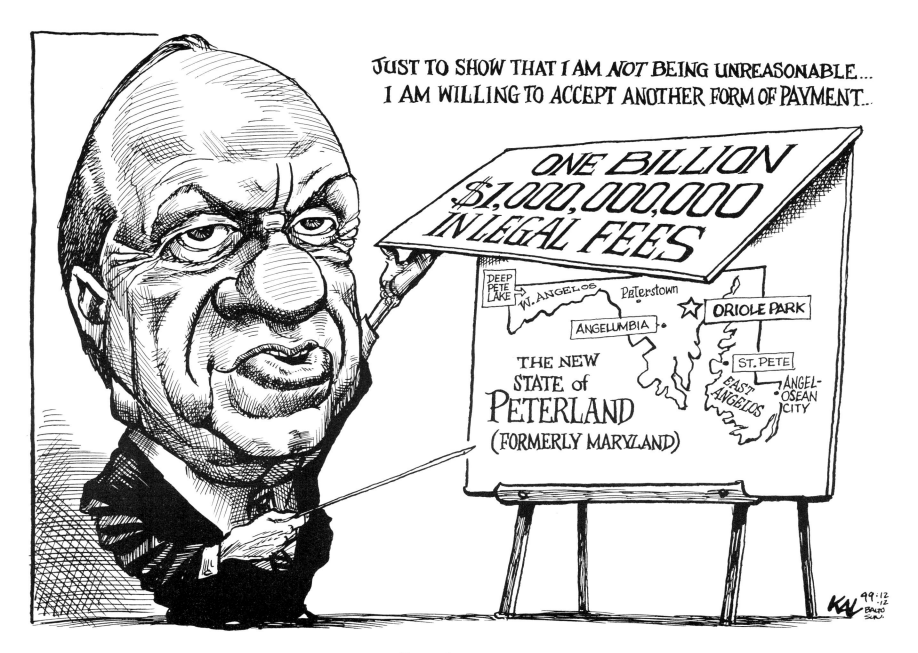

December 12, 1999

Peter Angelos won a tobacco settlement, but couldn't agree with state officials on the fee he was owed.

April 9, 2000
The governor got the legislature to pass a bill requiring safety locks on guns ...

SPEAKING OF GUN LOCKS

April 2, 2000
... despite strong opposition by the gun lobby.

149

March 29, 1997
Funding for Baltimore schools continued to be an issue in Annapolis.

November 23, 1997

About 1,200 students were suspended after defying their principal at a Baltimore high school.

November 16, 1997
Baltimore confirmed its position as the city that reads ... poorly.

February 6, 1999

Problems in court administration allowed some criminals to avoid prosecution.

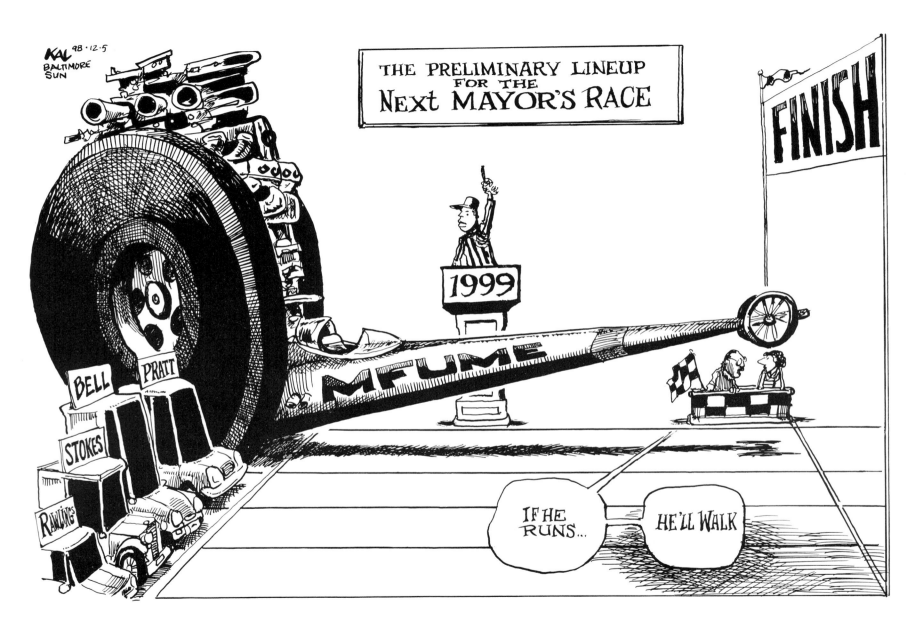

December 5, 1999

Kweisi Mfume, head of the NAACP, was an early favorite in the 1999 mayoral election, but he declined to run.

June 24, 1999
Crime, not surprisingly, was a key issue in the campaign.

September 4, 1999
There was little debate over the city's fiscal problems.

August 22, 1999

When early favorite Lawrence Bell spent campaign money on New York outfits, it didn't polish his image.

November 7, 1999
Martin O'Malley was elected, and inherited a mixed legacy.

October 30, 1999
O'Malley's crime-fighting plans stirred worries about over-zealous policing ...

April 1, 2000
... and led to a confrontation and the abrupt resignation of his first police commissioner.

May 16, 1999

Baltimore's own hit television program, "Homicide," was killed off.

March 29, 1998
Consequences followed the signing of $65 million outfielder Albert Belle.

January 10, 1998
The suburbs were often less than sympathetic to urban problems.

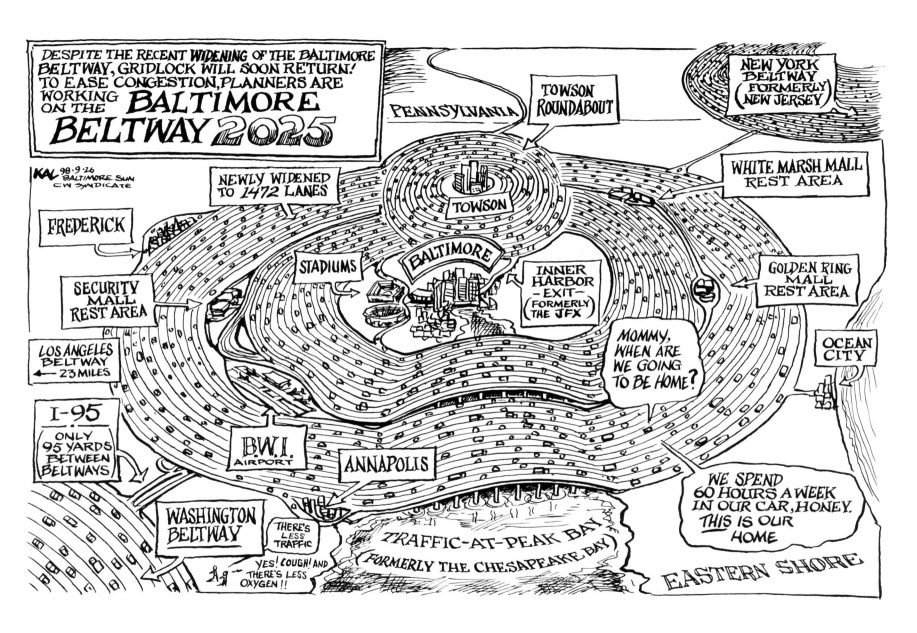

September 26, 1998
The Beltway was widened, but commuters hardly noticed.

About the cartoonist

Kevin Kallaugher (KAL) is the political cartoonist for *The Baltimore Sun* and *The Economist* magazine of London.

After graduating from Harvard College in 1977, Kevin joined the Brighton Basketball Club in England as a player and coach. The club hit financial difficulties, and Kevin began to draw caricatures of tourists. In 1978, *The Economist* recruited him to become its first resident cartoonist in its 145 year history.

Kevin returned to the U.S. in 1988 to join *The Sun* as its political cartoonist. He continues to draw three cartoons per week for *The Economist*. Kevin is also a regular contributor to *Business Central Europe* of Vienna.

KAL's work for *The Sun* and *The Economist*, distributed by Cartoonists & Writers Syndicate, has appeared in more than 100 publications worldwide, including *Le Monde, Der Spiegel, Pravda, Krokodil, Daily Yomiuri, The Australian, The New York Times, Time, Newsweek,* and *The Washington Post*.

Kevin's numerous awards include the 1999 Thomas Nast Award from the Overseas Press Club of America, the 1990 award for Best Editorial Cartoon at the Witty World International Cartoon Festival in Budapest, Hungary and the 1982 Feature Cartoonist of the Year Award from the Cartoonist Club Of Great Britain.

In 1995, Kevin curated the celebrated exhibit at The Walter's Art Gallery, "Worth a Thousand Words: A Picture of Contemporary Political Satire." He is past President of the Association of American Editorial Cartoonists and has had one-man exhibitions in London, New York, Washington and Baltimore.

Acknowledgements

The cartoonist and author thanks publisher Michael Waller and editorial page editor Jacqueline Thomas for their editorial support over the years. A particular thanks goes to Bill Salganik who acted as editor for this book. It was a pleasure working with someone with such a good understanding and appreciation of the tasks and goals of editorial cartooning.

Thanks, too, goes to Jeff Bill for his time and patience in taking the photographs for the cover illustration.

The author would like to gratefully acknowledge Mike Golden for facilitating Governor Schaefer's introduction.

Finally, thanks to the staff of SunSource for their welcoming embrace of this project. A special thank you goes to Jennifer Halbert, who designed and stage managed this book with skill, creativity and good humor.